This Book Belongs To:

_____

How To Draw 99 Cute Things
by Steve Herman

ISBN: 978-1-64916-155-0

www.MyDragonBooks.com

First Edition: April 2024
10 9 8 7 6 5 4 3 2 1

HOW TO DRAW
99 CUTE THINGS

STEVE HERMAN

Hey there, fellow artist!

It's me, Drew, and guess who's here with me?

Yep, my dragon, Piggory Doo!

We've got a super cool mission for you today.
You're going to learn how to draw 99 adorable things!

And guess what?
Each one comes with a fun fact!
Because learning
cool stuff rocks, right?

WHAT YOU NEED

Grab your pencil
and an eraser!

Make sure your pencil
is nice and sharp
for those
smooth lines!

And your eraser?
Well, it's your little
secret weapon for
any oopsies
you might make
along the way!

HOW TO DRAW

1. Start Simple

We're gonna start with easy, gentle lines. Imagine you're drawing with a feather - super light and breezy. This way, if we need to fix something, it's a piece of cake!

2. Follow The Leader

See those arrows?  They're like the treasure map leading us to our finished drawing. Follow them step by step, and you'll be amazed at what you can create.

3. Make it pop

Once you've got the basics down, press a bit harder with your pencil to make your drawing stand out. Those first lines were just our practice runs.

4. Your Turn

You will see a blank space on each page (like below)... That's your stage, your moment to shine! Try drawing what we just learned! Practice makes perfect!

Let's Have Fun! Have a blast with it! Drawing is all about letting your imagination fly!

Oh, and don't forget the grand finale - coloring your masterpiece!
After you're done drawing, grab your favorite colors
and bring your art to life.
Coloring isn't just fun; it makes your drawings truly yours.

Ready to start our drawing adventure?
Let's dive in and bring those cute things to life!
Catch you on the drawing side!

CONTENTS

Whale › 51	Baby Giraffe › 71	Pencil › 91
Baby Kangaroo › 52	Dragonfly › 72	Clock › 92
Baby Koala › 53	Grasshopper › 73	Shoe › 93
Monkey › 54	Ant › 74	Ball › 94
Zebra › 55	Beetle › 75	Umbrella › 95
Hippopotamus › 56	Polar Bear › 76	Bread › 96
Lion Cub › 57	Armadillo › 77	Blueberry › 97
Tiger Cub › 58	Dragon › 78	Peach › 98
Bear Cub › 59	Dinosaur › 79	Blackberry › 99
Beaver › 60	Cupcake › 80	Papaya › 100
Chipmunk › 61	Puzzle › 81	Pear › 101
Seal › 62	Bubble › 82	Apple › 102
Sea Turtle › 63	House › 83	Banana › 103
Lobster › 64	Tree › 84	Strawberry › 104
Crab › 65	Car › 85	Orange › 105
Shrimp › 66	Sunflower › 86	Watermelon › 106
Squid › 67	Cloud › 87	Pineapple › 107
Baby Goat › 68	Bicycle › 88	Grapes › 108
Calf › 69	Hat › 89	Cherry › 109
Baby Rhino › 70	Boat › 90	Kiwi › 110

KITTEN

Kittens can purr when they are only a few days old. ~~~ ♡

BABY PENGUIN

START

FINISH

GO!

Baby penguins are called chicks and are often covered in fluffy feathers.

CHICK

Little chicks start talking to their mom before they even hatch from their eggs.

GO!

20

GOLDFISH

23

TURTLE

START

Some turtles can breathe through their butts, a process known as cloacal respiration.

FINISH

SNOWFLAKE

Every snowflake has a unique pattern, no two are exactly alike.

GIRAFFE

A giraffe's tongue can be up to 18 inches long and is purplish-black in color.

PANDA

Pandas can eat 26 to 84 pounds of bamboo every day.

FROG

Frogs don't need to drink water as they absorb it through their skin.

33

OWL

Owls can rotate their heads as much as 270 degrees.

RABBIT

Rabbits can see almost all around them without turning their heads.

SQUIRREL

Squirrels help plant trees because they forget where they hide their nuts.

STARFISH

START

FINISH

If a starfish loses an arm, it can grow a new one back.

CLOWNFISH

Clownfish, like Nemo, are all born boys, and some become girls later.

41

RED PANDA

Red pandas use their fluffy tails to keep warm and to balance when they climb.

GUINEA PIG

Guinea pigs love to chat and play with their friends.

PARROT

START

FINISH

Parrots are smart birds that can learn to talk like people.

FLAMINGO

Baby flamingos are gray, but they turn pink from eating shrimp.

PEACOCK

Boys are called peacocks and girls are peahens. They have big, colorful feathers.

OTTER

Otters hold hands when they sleep so they don't drift away from each other.

48

OCTOPUS

JELLYFISH

Jellyfish don't have brains, but they can still swim and find food.

WHALE

The blue whale is the largest animal ever, even bigger than dinosaurs!

BABY KANGAROO (JOEY)

START

FINISH

GO!

Baby kangaroos are called joeys and live in their mom's pouch.

52

BABY KOALA

Baby koalas are also called joeys and are the size of jellybeans when they're born.

MONKEY

Some monkeys have tails so strong they can hang from them like a tree branch.

54

ZEBRA

Every zebra has a unique pattern of black and white stripes, just like human fingerprints.

HIPPOPOTAMUS

Hippos spend most of their day in water to keep their big bodies cool.

LION CUB

START

FINISH

GO!

Baby lions, called cubs, start to roar when they are about two years old.

BEAR CUB

Baby bears, called cubs,
love to climb trees.

BEAVER

Beavers use their big teeth to cut down trees and build homes called lodges.

CHIPMUNK

Chipmunks have cheek pouches to store food for later.

~ SEAL ~

Seals can sleep underwater and only come up for air.

SEA TURTLE

Sea turtles have been around since the time of the dinosaurs.

LOBSTER

Lobsters can live to be over 100 years old.

CRAB

Crabs have ten legs, but the front two are usually big claws.

SHRIMP

Shrimp can swim backward really fast.

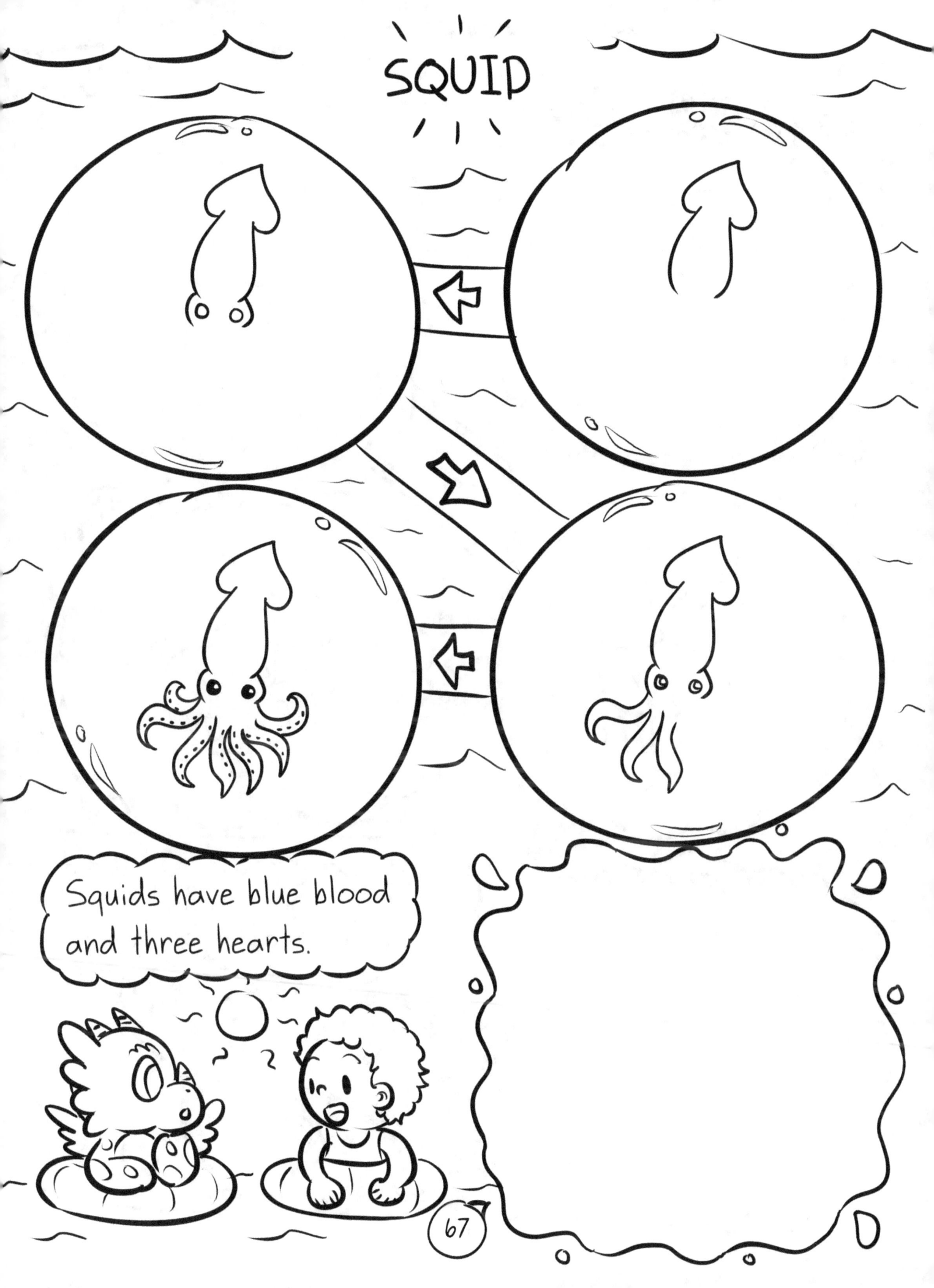

CALF

START

FINISH

A baby cow is called a calf, and they can walk very soon after birth.

A baby rhino is born without a horn; it starts to grow later.

BABY GIRAFFE

Baby giraffes can stand up and walk within an hour of being born.

71

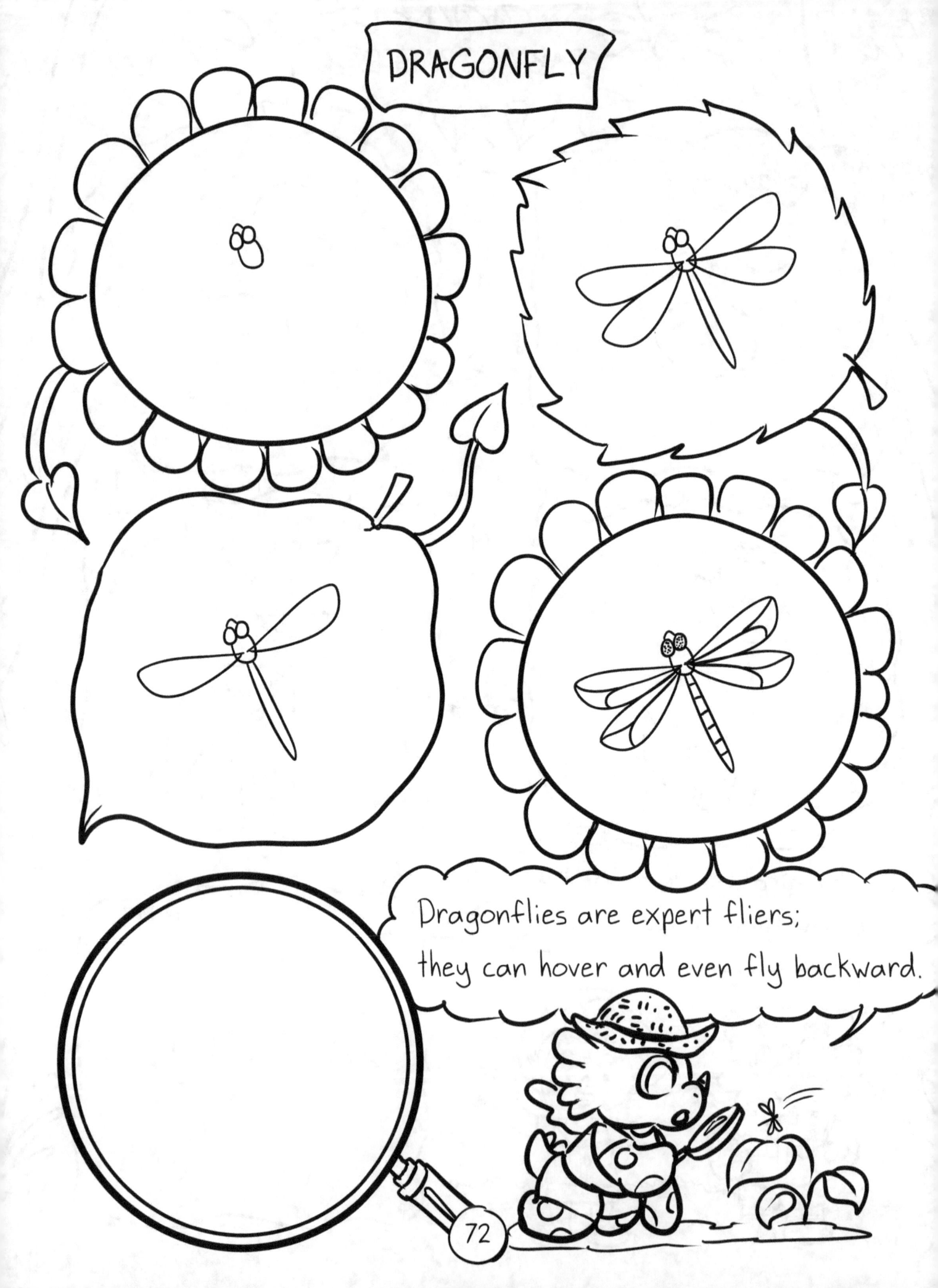

DRAGONFLY

Dragonflies are expert fliers; they can hover and even fly backward.

ANT

Ants can lift and carry more than three times their own weight.

BEETLE

Beetles have hard shells over their wings called elytra.

DINOSAUR

START

FINISH

Dinosaurs were huge, ancient animals;

79

CUPCAKE

The world's largest cupcake weighed over 2,500 pounds.

PUZZLE

GO!

Puzzles have been around for a long time – more than 250 years ago.

81

HOUSE

Houses are built with a variety of materials depending on local climate and availability.

TREE

Trees can 'talk' to each other underground through a network of fungi in the soil, often called the "Wood Wide Web."

CAR

START

FINISH

GO!

The first electric cars were made before cars with gasoline.

CLOUD

Clouds can weigh hundreds of tons, even though they appear light and fluffy.

87

BICYCLE

The first bicycles didn't have pedals; riders had to push themselves along the ground with their feet.

88

BOAT

START

FINISH

Boats float by pushing water out of the way.

90

PENCIL

Pencils can write underwater and in zero gravity.

CLOCK

The first mechanical clocks didn't have clock faces but struck bells to tell time.

92

SHOE

START

FINISH

The world's oldest surviving shoes are over 5,500 years old and were found in Armenia.

93

BALL

Balls have been used in games and sports for over 3,000 years.

94

UMBRELLA

Umbrellas were originally designed to shade people from the sun, not for rain.

BLUEBERRY

Blueberries can help improve your memory.

PEACH

BLACKBERRY

Blackberries are not really berries; each little bump in the "berry" is a fruit.

99

PAPAYA

100

PEAR

Pears ripen faster when placed next to bananas.

APPLE

There are over 7,500 varieties of apples worldwide.

STRAWBERRY

1

2

3

4

GO!

Strawberries are the only fruit with seeds on the outside.

104

ORANGE

Oranges are a type of berry called a "hesperidium."

WATERMELON

Watermelons are 92% water and were first grown in Egypt.

PINEAPPLE

It takes almost 3 years for a single pineapple to grow and ripen.

GRAPES

GO!

Grapes are used to make raisins, grape juice, jelly, and wine.

CHERRY

Cherry trees can produce fruit for up to 100 years. ~~~ ♡

Hey there, awesome artists!

You did it! Wow, we have so much fun drawing with you!

We hope you loved each of your creations as much as we loved showing you how!

Each page brought a new friend to life, and with every line and shade,

your skills have grown!

Don't stop here – keep drawing, imagining, and adding color

to your creations. Every artist started just like you.

So, keep at it, practice a lot, and most importantly,

have fun with your drawings!

The more you draw, the more magical your world becomes.

Bye for now!

www.ingramcontent.com/pod-product-compliance
Lightning Source LLC
Chambersburg PA
CBHW081533140526
45085CB00057B/531